THE FIRST THIRTY DAYS TO BECOMING A DISCIPLE MAKING CHURCH

KEN ADAMS

The First Thirty Days to Becoming a Disciple Making Church
impactdisciples.com

Copyright ©2021 by Ken Adams

Scripture quotations are from the ESV® Bible (The Holy Bible, English Standard Version®), copyright © 2001 by Crossway, a publishing ministry of Good News Publishers. Used by permission. All rights reserved.

All rights reserved. No part of this publication may be reproduced, stored in a retrieval system, or transmitted in any form or by any means - electronic, mechanical, photocopy, recording, or any other - except for brief quotations in printed reviews, without prior permission of the publisher.

Written by Ken Adams
Designed by Grace Asnip
Edited by Valeria Adams

Before you begin....

Let's be clear from the start. You can't become a disciple making church in thirty days, but you can learn a great deal of what it takes to be a disciple making church, and you can start planning how to become one in thirty days. This book can help you begin that process.

This thirty day booklet was written out of thirty years of trial and error. As a pastor of a local Body of Christ, I have made it my goal for the past thirty-one years to figure out how to lead a local church to become a movement of multiplying disciples. I still have not fulfilled that goal, but I have seen progress and I have learned volumes.

I write this booklet in an attempt to share with you some of what I have learned from God's word along with my own personal experience. I often say, I could write a book on "How not to be a movement of multiplying disciples". However, this booklet will give me an opportunity to share with you some of the important lessons I have learned and experienced along the way. I hope it will serve in some ways as a primer for leading churches to become disciple making churches.

I once heard it said, "That Jesus started the church the way he wanted it and now he wants it the way he started it." For years I have tried to find out who I heard make that statement. I can't find it anywhere, but it is still one of the most powerful statements I have ever heard. I believe Jesus started the church to be a movement of multiplying disciples, and I am swinging with all I've got to help lead at least one local church to become one.

The next thirty days will give you many solid principles taken from the life of Christ on how to do the very things Jesus did. And, as I am sure you agree, you can never go wrong doing what Jesus did. In fact, we want Jesus to be our model for life and ministry. If we don't see it in Jesus, it doesn't matter if we do it or not. If, however, we see it in Jesus, we most certainly need to see it in us! This booklet is for everyone and anyone, but I highly encourage that you work through it with a group of other believers. Every week has a discussion guide for use with a small group. if you read each lesson, dig in to the scriptures, and discuss each week with others, I believe you will drain this little booklet for all its worth. I pray that happens.

Being and Building Disciples,

Ken Adams

DAY ONE

"A Huge Difference"

As you begin this study on becoming a disciple making church, let's start with a major distinction. There is a huge difference between a disciple making church and a church with discipleship.

A church with discipleship tends to see discipleship as simply another program that is added to the rest of the stuff the church is doing. Discipleship becomes one of several options that people can choose from. It is usually seen as a program designed to help people "go deeper" or to master spiritual disciplines in their life. It is not the same thing as a disciple making church.

The disciple making church understands that disciple making is not another optional program of the church; it is the mission of the church! Making disciples is what the church does, it is not one of many things the church **can do.** In Matthew 28:19 Jesus told his disciples to *"Go therefore and make disciples of all nations..."* Making disciples is the end product of the church and all other activities are done in order to fulfill that mission. In the end, there is no other mission the church should be focusing on besides making disciples!

A disciple making church is a church that sees outreach efforts, worship services, small groups meetings, serving opportunities, and leadership development as parts of a whole. The whole church working together to create an environment where disciples can be made. Let me reiterate: Making disciples **is** the mission of Christ's church!

Every church should ask this fundamental question: Are we a church with discipleship or a disciple making church? An honest answer is the place to start, and the answer will help you to establish the next steps. To become a movement of multiplying disciples is exactly the way Jesus started the church to begin with. If you are a disciple making church you will see disciples being made that build even more disciples. Are you seeing this in your church these days? Is this happening in your life these days? If not, it is time to make a change. Keep reading, help is on the way.

DIG DEEPER

Read the following scripture passage and write one insight you gleaned from it. **Mark 1:16-20**

___
___
___

DAY TWO

"Be Clear on the Mission"

The mission in any organization must be made clear. As someone once said, "If you forget you're why (mission), you will lose your way." This is certainly true for the Church of Jesus Christ. Christians must be crystal clear on what the mission of the church is. If believers do not know the mission Christ gave his church, we might possibly end up pursuing all the wrong things, and this is exactly what our enemy would want!

Please understand that the church only has one mission. Two thousand years ago, Jesus stood on a mountainside in Galilee and he stated very clearly what the church was called to do until his return. Write the mission of the church Jesus gave in Matthew 28:19-20.

_____
_____
_____
_____

What we call the Great Commission is the church's mission. It is not one of many options to choose from, it is the only option. It does not change from church to church, it is the same for every church, everywhere. Christ's last command is to be our first priority.

Dallas Willard once said, "Since making disciples is the main task of the church, every church ought to be able to answer two questions. What is our plan for making disciples of Jesus? Is our plan working?" If you do not have a plan for making disciples, you will have a difficult time fulfilling the mission.

Every church and every Christian needs to be laser focused on the Great Commission. We all need a great commitment to the Great Commission. If the church is not fulfilling the mission of making disciples, we are not doing the very thing Jesus did and told us to be doing. We cannot afford to be fuzzy on the mission.

Mission drift happens. The enemy is very clever at getting the church off of the mission. If we are not careful, we can make a good worship service the mission, building programs the mission, having sweet fellowship the mission or making more knowledge the mission. All of these things can be good but only if they lead to making more disciples. In the end, being clear on the mission is crucial, and for a mission this critical, we can't afford to "lose our way"!

DIG DEEPER

Read **Matthew 28:16-20** and write an insight or two from your reading.

_____
_____
_____

DAY THREE

"Define the Target"

Mission is the "why". Target is the "what". In Matthew 28 Jesus told his disciples to *"make disciples"*. In Luke 6:40 he told his disciples to make *"fully trained"* disciples. Write that verse in the following blanks.

_____

_____

_____

_____

The target of every church is to make disciples that are fully trained.

Having a target enables us to know what to aim for. If you have no target you will never know if you hit the right thing or not. Jesus defines the target of making disciples as a fully trained disciple. Since Jesus clearly defines the target, we know exactly what the target is and can know when we have hit it and when we haven't.

The fully trained disciple will look like *"his teacher"*. This tells us that if we are fulfilling the mission of making disciples we will be helping untrained seekers become fully trained disciples that look and act like Jesus. The mission of the church is to make disciples that look like Jesus in their character and conduct. Character is demonstrated by *who* you are and conduct is displayed by *what* you do.

Every church exists to be a place where people are becoming more like Christ in their character and conduct. The character of Christ is best summarized by Paul in Ephesians 5:22,23. This list of spiritual fruit is not a comprehensive list of Christ's character but it provides a short summary of what Christ like character looks like. It makes the development of character objective not merely subjective.

The conduct of Christ is demonstrated in the Gospel accounts by the priorities of Jesus' life. Several of these priorities are easily identifiable when you look at the conduct of the disciples in the very first church recorded in Acts 2:42-47. The church in Jerusalem did what the original disciples did, and the original disciples did what they saw Jesus doing. This makes the conduct of Christ very objective and not simply subjective.

Having very concrete pictures of what Christ's character and conduct look like makes it very easy to know if a church is hitting the right target or not. The church that is making "fully trained" disciples with the character and conduct of Christ is accomplishing the right mission.

DIG DEEPER

Read **Luke 6:37-42** and write an insight or two about what you read.

_____
_____
_____

DAY FOUR

"Demonstrating Christ like Character"

Most Christians would agree that every church ought to be helping people grow in Christ like character. If, however, you asked them what that looked like when it happened you might not get that much agreement, but I don't think that is the way God intended it to be. Christ like character should look the same way in every Christ follower throughout all of history. A disciple with Christ like character should look as much like Jesus in who they are today as they would have two thousand years ago.

In Galatians 5:22-23 Paul provides us with a great summary list of Christ like attributes. The nine fruit he describes are a summary of what it looks like when a person is fleshing out the character of Christ. Love, joy, peace, patience, kindness, goodness, faithfulness, gentleness, and self control are all evidences of a life that is being controlled by the Spirit of God.

When a person's character is being controlled by the Spirit of God it helps transform them into the image of the Son of God. The more loving, joyful, peaceful, patient, kind, good, faithful, gentle, and self controlled you are becoming, the more like Christ you will be. This type of transformation should be the norm rather than the exception of the Christian life.

When Jesus told his disciples to "make disciples of all nations" he did it so that the planet would be filled with people who are demonstrating the fruit of the Spirit. A world filled with people that demonstrate love, joy, peace, patience, kindness, goodness, faithfulness, gentleness, and self-control would almost be like having heaven on earth. Clearly, this is why Jesus created the concept of a world filled with local, disciple making churches that are helping people go from untrained to fully trained believers. The world needs disciples who are demonstrating the character of Christ!

The target for every church, everywhere, is to make disciples that have the character of Christ. If the fruit of the Spirit is the starting place, then we have a subjective means of knowing when Christ like character is being developed. Christ like character should not be based on some objective criteria of what Christ like attributes are based on our thoughts or opinions. Christ like character should be identifiable and measurable the same way in the life of every fully trained disciple.

Jesus wanted his characteristics to look the same in all twelve of his disciples. The goal was that they all looked "like [their] teacher": Jesus.

DIG DEEPER

Read **Mark 3:14** and **Acts 4:13** and make an observation or two about these two verses.

_____
_____
_____

DAY FIVE

"Demonstrating Christ like Conduct"

What if I took a whiteboard and a marker and started writing all the things that Jesus did while he was here on the planet? We would need a bigger whiteboard for sure! But on that list there would be some things that Jesus did that his disciples also did. There would also be some things on that list that not only his disciples did but their disciples did as well. Then there would be some things on that list that Jesus did, his disciples did, their disciples did, and disciples today should be doing. Those "things" are what we call the conduct of Christ.

The conduct of Christ is not a list of arbitrary, subjective behaviors that we might or might not choose to emulate. The conduct or behavior of Christ is a very subjective, definable, and measurable set of priorities that Jesus lived his life by and expected all of his disciples to model.

In fact, in Act 2:42-47 we have a summary description of how the very first group of disciples behaved in the Jerusalem church. We can identify six behaviors in this list and a seventh a few chapters later in Acts chapter six. These seven behaviors were true of the first church, the original disciples, and of Jesus himself. We, therefore, can conclude that these seven things ought to be true of us. In the Jerusalem church they all...

> *"Belonged" therefore we should be members!*
> *"Grew" therefore we should be maturing!*
> *"Served" so therefore we should be ministers!*
> *"Gave" so therefore we should be managers!*

"Worshipped" so therefore we should be magnifiers!
"Shared" so therefore we should be messengers!
"Reproduced" so therefore we should be multipliers!

If the church is helping people to become fully trained disciples that all have the conduct of Christ, we stand a better chance of getting the same results they saw in the Jerusalem church. Like the first church, every church ought to be experiencing growth rather than decline. We ought to be managing increase rather than decrease. That is the way Jesus started his church and now he wants it the way he started it.

Is your church developing disciples that have the seven marks of Christ like conduct?

DIG DEEPER

Read **1 Corinthians 11:1** and share the insights you observe from the truth of this verse.

_____
_____
_____

DAY SIX

"Determine the Strategy"

Nobody goes from an untrained seeker to a fully trained disciple by accident. People take steps to become more like Jesus because they are intentionally and strategically led and developed through a process or pathway of growth. This is exactly what Jesus did.

Jesus took twelve unschooled, ordinary men and he led them to become fully trained disciples that would give leadership to his mission and movement. These men were identified in Acts as "men who have turned the world upside down".That same process needs to be repeated over and over again today in order to keep Christ's mission and movement going. The church today needs to be strategically leading people to become world changers for Christ!

We need to be implementing the exact same strategy Jesus executed two thousand years ago. His plan will work, if we will only work his plan!

Jesus began the process of leading untrained seekers to become fully trained disciples by inviting people in the _culture into a crowd_. As Jesus connected with people through personal relationships he encouraged them to come and see what he had to offer.

Jesus invited people in his "Christ crowd" to step out of the _crowd and into community_. Jesus used a small group environment to encourage people to follow him and connect with him on a relational level.

Jesus also used a small group community to be the environment for building his discipleship core. He challenged the _community to become his core_ by remaining in his word which enabled him to build a team of potential leaders. It took Jesus approximately three years to lead the twelve out of the culture and into his core of disciples.

Jesus commissioned the _core to become the called_. Jesus sent out his fully trained disciples to be leaders of his movement. He knew that they were ready to drive his mission and lead the church to become a movement of multiplying disciples just as he had done with them.

Here is the really good news. This same strategy Jesus used two thousand years ago works today! The question is whether or not we are committed to working the strategy of Jesus?

DIG DEEPER

Read **John 20:20-23** and write down an insight or observation from what you read.

_____
_____
_____

DAY SEVEN

"From Culture to Crowd"

Every church needs a plan to invite the culture into a Christ crowd. The very first step in helping people become fully trained disciples came from a simple invitation. "Come and see". Jesus started the entire movement of Christianity as recorded by John 1:39 by inviting two of John's disciples, *"come and you will see"*. Those two disciples took Jesus up on his invitation and they eventually became leaders in his movement. They became world changers and helped to fulfill the mission of making disciples of all nations.

The mission and movement of Jesus continues today because we give people invitations to come and see who Christ is and what he can do in their life. In the first century all the "come and see" invitations were through personal relationships. People reached people. Today, people still reach people, but there are additional ways to connect with people. You might want to consider using the following "doors" to invite people to come and see.

<u>Special Days & Events</u>! Christmas and Easter are always big days when people are more likely to check out a church service. Events such as a Family Weekend or First Responders Recognition Sunday are events that can be planned to encourage people to invite others.

<u>Servant Projects or Random Acts of Kindness</u>! / Serving people in Jesus' name is a great way to connect with people and invite them to come and see, and there are hundreds of different ways to do

this. A water bottle give away, a gas buy down, or providing lunch for teachers are all examples of servant outreaches.

Discovery Groups! A Discovery Group is a special outreach small group where people are invited from the community to learn more about a certain topic or need in their life. That small group becomes a door for relationship building that can lead to a "come and see" invitation.

Mail and Social Media! A strong advertising plan using either traditional mail or social media is a great way to invite people to "come and see" what God is doing at your church.

All of the doors mentioned above are simply first steps to making a personal connection with people. Once a connection has been made and invite can be given. Every church ought to have an annual plan for inviting the culture into their Christ crowd.

DIG DEEPER

Read **John 1:29-39** and write down any insights or take aways you see from this passage.

_____
_____
_____

QUESTIONS FOR REFLECTION OR DISCUSSION

The past seven days have gotten you started on learning what it means to have a Disciple Making Church. Take a few minutes to reflect on the following questions or discuss them with others.

1- How would you describe the difference between a church with discipleship and a disciple making church? Which one is more true for your church?

2- What is the mission Christ gave to his church? How is your church doing at fulfilling Christ's mission?

3- Why is having a clearly defined target so important to a church? What was the clearly defined target for Jesus?

4- What is the difference between character and conduct and how were they displayed in the life of Christ?

5- Would you say the character and conduct of Christ is more subjective or objective? Explain your answer.

6- How did Jesus lead people from being untrained seekers to becoming fully trained disciples? How well is this happening in your church?

7- Does your church have an annual outreach plan? What kind of things could you do to invite more people to "come and see"?

DAY EIGHT

"Creating a Compelling Christ Crowd"

If you invite people to "come and see" guess what might happen? That's right, they might come to see. When they do, you need to make sure they have a genuine encounter with Christ. That's exactly what happened when Jesus invited untrained seekers to "come and see" in his ministry.

When Jesus started his earthly ministry John the Baptist looked at him and said, *"Behold the Lamb of God!"* This "come and behold" stage of helping untrained seekers become fully trained disciples is critical. Seekers usually find themselves as a part of a Christ crowd before they ever find themselves connected to community or serving. Being in a Christ crowd is a logical step in the process of becoming a fully trained disciple.

Since a Christ crowd is so important it needs to be compelling. It needs to be an experience that people will want to come back to. When Jesus spoke to crowds in his day the people were "amazed" or "astonished" at his teaching. if you want people in your Christ crowd to be amazed, I suggest you work on creating four "wow" experiences.

<u>A wow welcome</u>! Everyone is different and some like to be recognized when they visit a crowd and some like to remain anonymous. Make both options possible for your crowd guests. Give every new person a warm greeting and help them at the level they desire. Don't let them wander around feeling lost and alone!

Make them feel at home and be willing to answer whatever questions or concerns they may have.

A wow encounter! The best way to create a wow encounter in your Christ crowd is to lift up Jesus. If an adult, teenager, or child has a legitimate encounter with Christ, they will be wowed. Genuine worship and the relevant teaching of God's Word in an authentic environment is the best way to help people encounter Christ.

A wow environment! A nasty restroom is not a wow experience! An outdated and ugly church campus is not making your guest say, "wow". When Jesus fed the five thousand I bet someone said, "wow", this fish sure is good. Jesus took care of his crowds!

A wow follow-up! People want to be followed up the same way they are greeted. Some don't want any contact and some do. The best way to follow up with people is to give them choices. Make sure they understand there is a next step and how they can take it.

DIG DEEPER

Read **John 6:1-14** and write down any insights you might have.

_____
_____
_____

DAY NINE

"Invite the Crowd into Community"

Jesus spent time with crowds but he invited a few untrained seekers to join him in community. In John 1:43 he said to Philip, *"Follow me."* This call was offered to others as well. With this invitation Jesus was asking a handful of potential disciples to travel with him to the region of Galilee and thereby experience a deeper level of fellowship with him. Jesus was inviting those in the crowd to experience life changing community.

Jesus used a small group to be the place where his potential disciples joined him in community. They traveled together, ate together, learned together, and did ministry together. At this stage of development these men went from seekers and attenders to become members who were committed to following Jesus. These men were not yet considered leaders, but they were taking a next step and they were on the path to becoming fully trained disciples.

Once people become regular attenders in the "crowd" it is important to invite them to take a next step. Taking a next step is often referred to in today's church world as assimilation. Assimilation is the process of helping people get connected and become a part of the local church community. It is a dis-service to not help someone take a next step and connect to life changing, biblical community.

You might want to create a "next steps" class that helps connect people in several ways.

Connect to a small group! Everyone needs to be in a small group. A small group is the perfect environment for fellowship to be developed and for caring and spiritual growth to happen. Every small group ought to be Bible-centric and small enough to emphasize personal relationships and care for one another.

Connect to a ministry team! Everyone needs to serve with others in ministry. Biblical community is not just receiving, it also involves giving. Life changing community needs to give people a way to contribute and make a difference for the kingdom's sake. Every believer needs to find a place to use their spiritual gift and God given ability to help others.

Connect to a growth process! We all need to have a map rather than a menu for our spiritual growth and development. Having a step by step plan for how to grow spiritually and become a fully trained disciple is essential for being connected to a local church.

DIG DEEPER

Read **Acts 2:41-47** and write down the observations about how believers were connected in the Jerusalem church.

_____
_____
_____

DAY TEN

"Encourage the Community to Become the Core"

The twelve men in Jesus' small group became his disciple making core when they began to grow and learn to live and lead like Jesus did. In the strategy of Jesus, the invitation to "follow me" eventually became a challenge to "abide in my word". Jesus had a plan to take these men deeper. His goal was to give them more than great fellowship, his goal was to transform their lives!

As the disciples began to abide, or obey the Word, they were transformed and became more like Jesus and less like themselves. They literally went from unschooled, ordinary men to fully trained disciples. This doesn't mean they were perfect, but it does mean they were equipped to fulfill the mission of Jesus and lead his movement.

The goal of having a disciple making core is not to help people master spiritual disciplines. The goal of a disciple making core is ministry training. Jesus was making disciples for a purpose. Jesus made disciples to fulfill the mission of reaching the world. It really is the master's plan of evangelism.

After three years of equipping the twelve, Jesus actually had twelve men that could live like he lived and could lead like he led. He had strategically and intentionally given them his character and conduct as a model to follow. Jesus had trained a handful of men that would in turn train others to have his character and conduct.

In order to build a disciple making core today, we need the same two things Jesus had. It really isn't as hard as you might think, you simply need to do it.

Disciple making requires a place! Jesus used the small group not only as a place for creating community, he also used it as a place for building a core of world changing disciples. The small group is always the primary place for developing disciples. Every disciple making church needs to have disciple making small groups.

Disciple making requires a plan! Jesus had an intentional plan to develop his disciples. He didn't have a course or book, but he did have a plan. He taught his disciples how to pray, how to serve others, how to witness, how to manage their resources, how to worship, how to make disciples, and the importance of scripture and the need for belonging. Not only did Jesus model those specific behaviors he also demonstrated the characteristics of love, joy, peace, patience, kindness, goodness, faithfulness, gentleness, and self control. Jesus was very strategic in his approach to making disciples.

DIG DEEPER

Read **Mark 6:30-31** and write down any insights you observe.

_____
_____
_____

DAY ELEVEN

"Commission the Core as the Called"

Jesus did not tell us to go make leaders. He told us to "go make disciples". Jesus spent approximately three years making disciples that would become his leadership team once he returned to heaven. Jesus' disciple making core became a team of called leaders who accepted Christ's commission. These "called" leaders made Christ's last command their first priority. We should be very glad they did!

Christ's called leaders kept the mission and movement of Jesus going. He passed the baton to them and they passed it to the next generation of Christ followers. This chain of disciple making has multiplied all over the world and has continued for over two thousand years. What an amazing plan this is in order to make disciples of all nations.

Every church needs a plan to develop and deploy called leaders. If you have a discipleship process that teaches the character and conduct of Christ, you have the right plan for development. Once disciples have been developed they must be deployed. Fully trained disciples must be sent out to make more disciples for the movement to continue. There are at least three essentials that must be shared to deploy leaders into the harvest.

<u>The called have a shared mission</u>! All of Jesus' disciples knew exactly what the mission was. They never debated the mission. Everyone of them knew they were called to make disciples that looked like Jesus.

The called have a shared strategy! When the disciples started making disciples each of them did it the exact same way. They made disciples the same way Jesus had discipled them. The disciple were united in their strategy of making disciples. No one had to figure out the disciple making process, they simply needed to do what Jesus did.

The called have a shared passion! Every disciple, except Judas, was equally bought in to the disciple making mandate of Jesus. They had a shared passion for the mission and movement of Christ and were all willing to give up their lives to see it accomplished.

When you have team of called leaders that share a mission, strategy, and passion you have a team that can turn the world upside down. Every church needs to have a team of **disciples** who are willing to answer the leadership call!

DIG DEEPER

Read **John 20:19-23** and record any insights you see in that passage.

_____
_____
_____

DAY TWELVE

"Design Disciple Making Environments"

We become like the environment we place ourselves in. If we want to get in shape physically, we might join a gym or fitness center. If we want to grow intellectually, we might enroll in a University or College. If we want to network and connect socially we might join a civic organization of club. The environment you place yourself in will have a direct correlation with the person you become.

If you want to be a disciple of Jesus Christ you need to place yourself in a disciple making environment. The God ordained environment for making disciples is the church. The family of God is the best place for making disciples in the same way the biological family is the best place for raising children. It is God's idea, not ours. It works when the environment is designed the way God desires it.

Within the church there are several environments. Every church has large group environments, small group environments, and ministry environments. The same was true for Jesus and his disciples. Jesus used all of these environments, but the primary environment for disciple making was a small group. Jesus used the small group to help shape the lives of twelve men who in turn would shape the world.

As we lead untrained seekers to become fully trained disciples, we invite them to step out of the crowd and into community. We then challenge those in community to commit to a disciple making small group we call the core. If order to design disciple making small groups to be like the group Jesus used, we need four ingredients:

Content! Jesus gave his disciples information. He taught them and he gave them life changing truth. Every disciple making small group needs to be centered in the Word of God. God's word changes lives.

Contact! Jesus spent time with his disciples. He built a relationship with each of them them. They traveled together, ate together, walked, talked, and laughed together. Every disciple making small group needs to have relational time.

Context! Jesus involved his disciples in ministry experiences. They didn't just talk about ministry, they did it together. Every disciple making small group should prioritize doing ministry together.

Correction! Jesus used the small group to transform his disciples. It was a place of correction and loving accountability. Every disciple making small group needs to be a place that helps people change.

DIG DEEPER

Read **Mark 3:13 and 14** and record any observations you have on this passage.

_____
_____
_____

DAY THIRTEEN

"Life Changing Content"

One of the most important things Jesus did to develop his disciples was to teach them. Jesus used the small group as a place to transfer truth to the twelve. Jesus taught his disciples things that they did not yet know. However, Jesus did not teach the disciples everything they *could* know, he only taught them what they needed to know. Jesus simply gave them the information they needed to accomplish the mission. Jesus came to make disciples, not theologians.

When we design small discipleship groups that look like Jesus' group, we must remember that they need content. They need to be centered around the Bible and especially the life and teachings of Jesus. In Acts 2:42 the Jerusalem believers were described as being, *"devoted to the apostles' teaching"*. The apostles' teaching was the teaching they had received from Jesus. The life and teachings of Jesus became the curriculum for disciple making in the very first church and should be the curriculum for us today.

Every disciple needs to be a life long learner of God's Word. We never graduate from biblical knowledge. The goal, however, of a disciple making small group, is too train disciples to become life long learners and equip them to live and lead like Jesus did. The disciple making core are those people who have been equipped with the character and conduct of Christ and are committed to fulfilling his mission of making more disciples.

As a basic minimum every fully trained disciple needs to be taught the character of Christ. The character of Christ can be summed up in the Fruit of the Spirit that Paul describes in

Galatians 5:22,23. Jesus taught his character through his example and the disciples caught it by being with him. We need to know the character of Christ by studying how Jesus dealt with people in the gospels.

A fully trained disciple also needs to be taught the conduct of Christ. The conduct of Christ can be found all throughout the gospels, and it is also clearly seen in the priorities of the church described in Acts 2:42-47. The behaviors that we see prioritized in the disciples of the church in Jerusalem are a great summary of the conduct Christ expects to see reproduced in each of us.

In Matthew 28:20 Jesus tells his disciple to make disciples by *"teaching them to observe all that I have commanded you."* Life changing content is a must for every small discipleship small group.

DIG DEEPER

Read **Mark 1:21-22** and make any observations that you might have.

_____
_____
_____

DAY FOURTEEN

"Life Changing Contact"

Maybe you have heard the statement, "more is always caught than taught"? That is certainly a true statement and it is certainly the case in disciple making. The disciples of Jesus caught as much from Jesus' actions as they did from his words. The disciples learned the character and conduct of Jesus simply by association with him. Disciple making requires content but it also requires contact. Disciples are made in relationships, not simply in a classroom.

Think about how much time Jesus spent with disciples in non-teaching environments. Jesus and his disciples walked everywhere they went. They ate together. They probably fished together. They laughed and told stories with each other. They simply did life together. We can only imagine how much the disciples caught from Jesus while they were in close contact with each other.

If you want to have maximum impact on your disciples, you need to meet with them in a group environment but you also need to connect with them in relational environments. You need to share meals together. Participate in recreational activities together. Maybe travel together. Simply do life together.

So many things can be taught when a disciple and a disciple maker are spending time with each other. The conversations that develop become the agenda for what needs to be discussed. Many times in the relational times the real needs arise and the most important subjects can be dealt with. Often things are talked through in a casual, relational environment that might never come up in a group with a curriculum. According to John 21:25, *"there [were] also many other things that Jesus did"* that were never written down, so we don't even have a written record of all the things Jesus and his disciples may have discussed while spending time with each other.

Never underestimate the power of contact or association. In 1 Corinthians 15:33, Paul says, *"Do not be deceived: Bad company ruins good morals."* Paul is stressing the power of association in our lives. I believe the opposite of what Paul is saying is also true. I believe, good company builds good morals. Remember, more is always caught than taught.

We become like the people we surround ourselves with, so we need to surround ourselves with people who are pursuing the character and conduct of Christ. Our contact with them will shape who we are and what we do. This is disciple making.

DIG DEEPER

Read **Luke 11:1** and describe how association impact the disciples.

_____
_____
_____

QUESTIONS FOR REFLECTION OR DISCUSSION

The past seven days have helped you understand more of what it means to have a Disciple Making Church. Take a few minutes to reflect on the following questions or discuss them with others.

1- Spend a few minutes reviewing Jesus' strategy for helping people move from untrained seekers to fully trained disciples.

2- What should we hope happens to a person when the step out of the culture into a Christ crowd? How can your church improve the Christ crowd you have each weekend?

3- How and why did Jesus establish community with his followers and how does your church do the same today?

4- Describe the difference between community and core in Jesus' strategy and how does a disciple making core need to look today?

5- How did Jesus develop leaders and what are some key components of leadership development?

6- What are some of the environments Jesus put his disciples in and how important is environment for spiritual development?

7- Explain the difference between content and contact and how both play a role in making disciples that are fully trained.

DAY FIFTEEN

"Life Changing Context"

One of my favorite classes in college was Anatomy and Physiology. The reason I enjoyed it so much was because of the laboratory part of the class. Like many science classes this class had both a lecture and a lab. We sat in a classroom and listened to our professor teach about the human body three times a week, but twice a week we went into a laboratory and got practical experience dissecting different animals. Disgusting, I know.

The best part of the lab experience, however, was the day we visited a human cadaver laboratory. It was amazing! We examined human bodies and parts of bodies in such a way that it allowed you to see so much more than a textbook or a professor's words could ever provide. We got practical application of the information that we had read about and heard taught.

Disciple making also involves the application of the information you read in God's Word. That's called "context". Context is when you apply what you have learned in the group, outside the group. Context is when you share your faith with someone because you have studied what it means to be a messenger. Context is when you take a meal to someone who is struggling because you have learned what it means to be a minister.

Jesus used context in the way he went about training the twelve. Jesus took his disciples with him when he met with sinners and tax collectors at Matthew's house. Jesus had his disciples with him when he healed people and fed the multitudes. They learned how to live and lead like Jesus by watching him, not simply by listening to him!

I believe that context is the number one missing ingredient in disciple making today. We are missing one of the most important ingredients Jesus used in making disciples. We like to sit in circles in church buildings and we rarely ever go out and do what we are talking about inside those circles. That is the equivalent of learning to fish by watching a video on the internet. The best way to learn to fish is at a lake with a rod and reel in your hand.

The most effective way to make a disciple is to use content, contact, and context. Using all three of these ingredients is the way Jesus made disciples and it is a well rounded approach to helping people become fully trained disciples. Remember, we learn from what we hear, what we see, but also from what we do.

DIG DEEPER

Read **Mark 2:13-17** and write one or two insights from the passage.

_____
_____
_____

DAY SIXTEEN

"Life Changing Correction"

One of the most overlooked ingredients of a disciple making small group is the fact that it is the ideal place to help bring about "correction" in the life of a disciple. Jesus didn't just see the small group as a place to give content, contact, and context, he also saw it as the primary place to confront his disciples in a loving way and hold them accountable for their actions. As a result, the disciples experienced radical, life transformation.

Remember that Jesus' disciples started out as uneducated, common men. They had their issues and baggage that came from just being regular old guys. Over a period of three years Jesus challenged their lack of faith, their fears, their selfishness, and their lack of understanding to the point that their lives changed. These uneducated, common men became world changers and led the movement of Christ after he was gone.

Jesus helped these men change by coming to the end of themselves. He confronted the problem with self and called them to "come and die". In John 12:24 Jesus says, *"Truly, truly, I say to you, unless a grain of wheat falls into the earth and dies, it remains alone; but if it dies, it bears much fruit."* Once a person comes to the end of themself they can be transformed and live a life that bears much fruit.

Making disciples is messy. People have broken relationships, damaged emotions, unhealthy habits, sinful thoughts, and a host of other issues that prevent them from being who God wants them to be and doing what God wants them to do. As they are exposed to the Truth of God, experience the Spirit of God, and engage with the People of God over time they are transformed into the image of the Son of God.

A small discipleship group like Jesus had is the ideal environment for transformation. God can actually use the other people in the group to shape and mold you into his image. Some of those people are sandpaper people and some are velvet people. God uses both types of people in your life to help make you into the person you were created to be.

John the Baptist said it best in John 3:30, *"He must increase, but I must decrease."* The more you decrease and the more Christ increases in you, the more you will become like Christ and display his character and his conduct. Becoming a fully trained disciple requires correction, but the end result is a man or woman who looks a lot more like Jesus.

DIG DEEPER

Read **Mark 9:33-35** and write any observations you have regarding this passage.

_____
_____
_____

DAY SEVENTEEN

"Develop Disciple Making Leaders"

Jesus told us to "make disciples", not leaders. He said this because a commitment to making disciples will increase your pool of potential leaders more than any other method. Jesus made disciples, and then he appointed leaders, and we must do the same.

I can't begin to tell you how many Pastors have told me that their number one greatest need in their church is more leaders. When I ask them how they plan to meet that need, most of them have absolutely no plan. The truth is, many are just hoping good leaders will transfer to their church from some other church. But, there is a better way!

Jesus did not have leaders join his team from another church. Jesus developed his leaders out of discipleship. In other words, Jesus was very intentional about helping untrained seekers, the disciples, grow up to become called leaders that he would send out to make more fully trained disciples. Jesus spent three years developing disciples that could take over the leadership of his mission and movement.

When Jesus completed his training of his disciples, he knew he had developed "ready" disciple making leaders. These disciples were ready to become leaders because they had been trained by the master developer. Jesus had spent three years developing leaders the way God describes them in Jeremiah 3:15, *"And I will give you shepherds after my own heart, who will feed you with knowledge and understanding."* A shepherd is a leader, so every disciple making leader ought to have the same qualities.

The right heart! Jesus made disciples that became leaders that had hearts after God. In other words, they desired and were driven by the same things Jesus was driven by. A disciple making leader will desire to see every person, in every nation, in every generation be and build disciples of Christ.

The right knowledge! Jesus made sure his disciples became leaders that knew how to lead the way he did. They knew the priorities of a leader. They knew how to live like Jesus did. They knew how to lead like Jesus did, and they knew how to leverage their influence the way Jesus did.

The right understanding! Jesus made sure his disciples understood how to lead others the same way he led others. Jesus made sure they understood the power of a shared mission, shared strategy, and shared passion.

DIG DEEPER

Read **Matthew 9:37-38** and write down any insights you observe.

_____
_____
_____

DAY EIGHTEEN

"Develop Leaders with the Right Heart"

Here is one of the most important principles I have learned after thirty years of leading a local church. If you have leaders with the right heart everything else will work right, but if you have leaders with the wrong heart nothing will work right.

I say this because if the heart, (the "desire"), of a leader is the same as God's desire, there is no problem you can't come together to solve. If, on the other hand, the desire of the leader does not line up with the heart of God, you will have trouble coming together on just about everything. A room full of leaders that all have "hearts after God" will always end up going in the same direction which will be God's direction.

Having a heart after God means having the same "desire" that Jesus had. The heart is what drives a person. It is the thing that makes a person do what they do. We often say to a child, "do it with all your heart". Or we might say, "put your heart into it". These sayings refer to a person having the right desire. It means being driven by the right thing.

When we say a leader has a "heart after God" it means that leader is driven or desires the same things God desires and is driven by. Jesus left the majesty, glory, and splendor of heaven to come to this stinky, slimy, place called earth to see every person, in every nation, learn what it means to be and build disciples of Christ. This mission is literally what drove Jesus to do all that he did.

Just imagine having an entire team of leaders that share the heart of God. One of Jesus' main objectives while training the twelve was to give them a heart after God. He wanted them to change their desires. His goal was to help them go from fishing for fish to fishing for men. Jesus wanted to give them a desire and be driven by his mission. The longer they were with him the more they began to have the same desires he had.

Transforming the heart does not happen over night. No one accepts Christ and then automatically changes their heart's desire. Over time, the Spirit of God combined with the Word of God in the context of the People of God transforms a person's heart. This is why I say, "the best leadership comes out of discipleship".

If a church is serious about developing leaders it must be making disciples that have a desire to see every person, in every nation, and every generation be and build disciples of Christ.

DIG DEEPER

Read **Proverbs 4:23** and make a note or two about what this verse says to you personally.

_____
_____
_____

DAY NINETEEN

"Develop Leaders with the Right Knowledge"

Recently I was part of a luncheon with about seventy-five pastors. The question was asked how many of those pastors had ever been discipled? Less than half the pastors in that room raised their hands! Here in lies one of the greatest problems with the church today. If we have leaders that do not know the things they need to know about leading a disciple making church, then we will have a hard time fulfilling that mission.

Over a period of three years Jesus taught his disciples three very specific things they needed to know in order to lead his mission and his movement. These three priorities of leadership were essential for them to be the leaders they needed to be. Jesus taught them how to live like he lived. He taught them how to lead like he led. Jesus taught his disciples how to leverage their influence like he leveraged his.

The disciples became qualified leaders because they knew Christ's character and conduct. They knew who he was and what he did and they knew that his character and conduct should also be true of them. The disciples were far from perfect, but they did know how they were supposed to live. If they lived like Jesus lived, they would be the right kind of leaders.

The disciples became qualified leaders because they led others the same way Jesus led them. In three years Jesus had intentionally and strategically led his disciples to go from untrained seekers to fully trained disciples. The disciples knew how to lead people because they had seen it modeled right in front of them. They could lead well because they had been led well.

Finally, the disciples knew how to leverage their influence through others. Jesus had taught them how to become leaders of leaders. They learned this by seeing Jesus leverage his influence through them. Jesus' disciples were not just leaders, they were leaders of leaders. Knowing the priority of leveraging your influence qualifies you to be a disciple making leader.

Jesus could launch his disciples into leadership because he was confident they knew exactly what they needed to know. They had received the right knowledge for leading. Jesus was literally sending out Jeremiah 315 leaders to be on mission for him. Today we need leaders in the church that are disciple making leaders. We need leaders that have the knowledge to lead like Jesus led.

DIG DEEPER

Read **Luke 10:1-24** and make any observations about how Jesus developed his disciples into qualified leaders.

_____
_____
_____

DAY TWENTY

"Develop Leaders with the Right Understanding"

Believe it or not there are a lot of people in leadership that simply don't understand how to lead. They have a mission, a strategy, and passion but they don't have a clue how to share any of this with other people. A movement will never get started unless a leader understands how to share what they are doing with other people.

The success in Jesus' leadership was his understanding of how to get others to do what he did and live like he lived. His disciples shared his mission, his strategy, and his passion. That is what caused Christianity to become a movement of multiplying disciples. If Jesus had not been able to pass on what he was doing to others the movement of Christianity would have stopped with Jesus. The success of Christianity totally rested in Jesus' understanding of how to lead others.

Jeremiah 3:15 describes it this way, *"And I will give you shepherds after my own heart, who will feed you with knowledge and understanding."* Jesus was a 315 leader because he had the understanding needed to get his disciples to share what he had. Jesus had the right heart, right knowledge, and right understanding and he passed all three to his disciples.

Every disciple making leader needs to understand the power of "sharing". It is a shared mission that has power. It is a shared strategy that causes momentum. It is a shared passion that creates excitement in a group of people. When a leader understands how to share with others, movements grow and missions are fulfilled.

The Book of Acts is evidence of Jesus' leadership. Acts shows us the church shared the mission of Jesus. The church shared the strategy of Jesus. The church shared the passion of Jesus. This is exactly why the church grew from 120 people to thousands in less than forty years. The church did not grow by accident, it grew because of leadership. Christ shared with the apostles and they shared with others who then shared it with others.

If a leader wants to be successful, he or she will need to understand how to get multiple generations of disciples buying into the cause. Failure to get buy-in from others will make the movement stall and eventually die.

Jesus made disciples and developed them into leaders by selecting the right people, equipping them to lead, and launching them into ministry. This same process is needed today. Every church needs a plan to make 315 leaders.

DIG DEEPER

Read **Jeremiah 3:11-18** and make write down any observations you see in this passage.

_____
_____
_____

DAY TWENTY-ONE

"Develop Leaders for the Right Results"

Whenever you make fully trained disciples and appoint them to be disciple making leaders you will get the right results regarding the mission. The mission will increase rather than decrease! Let me show how true that statement is.

In Acts 2:42-47 we have a snapshot of how the church was operating shorty after Jesus had ascended back to heaven. If you read carefully you will see that the church was experiencing great growth. They had more people joining the movement, not less. They had more people in public worship, not less. They had more people in small home groups, not less. They had more people growing in their faith, not less. They had more people caring and serving others, not less. They had more people managing their resources to serve God and others, not less. They had more people sharing the message of Christ, not less. If you read ahead to Acts 6:7 you will see that they had more disciples being multiplied, not less. My guess is every pastor and leader would love to see those same types of results in their church?

The church in Acts was increasing rather than decreasing because Jesus had left leaders in charge that had the right heart, the right knowledge, and the right understanding. When you have disciple making 315 leaders, you will always get the right results. It is true, everything really does rise and fall on leadership. If you have developed disciple making leaders, you will have a disciple making church. If you develop another type of leader, who knows what type of church you will have? It probably will not be a church that is fulfilling the mission of making disciples.

A church that does not have a discipleship process that produces disciple making leaders is like a military that never teaches their soldiers how to shoot a gun. It is like a school system that never teaches their teachers how to read. It is like an athletic organization that never trains their athletes to play the game. Churches that make disciples are led by churches that develop disciple making leaders. The question is, what type of plan does your church have in place that develops more and more disciple making leaders?

Always remember that a movement will only expand as fast as its leadership can be developed. If you want to see the church expand as a movement of multiplying disciples, you must be continually developing leaders. Make this a priority.

DIG DEEPER

Read **Acts 6:1-7** and record an insight or two from this text.

_____
_____
_____

QUESTIONS FOR REFLECTION OR DISCUSSION

The past seven days have helped you understand more of what it means to have a Disciple Making Church. Take a few minutes to reflect on the following questions or discuss them with others.

1- Take a minute and review the four main elements that make a disciple making church.

2- Explain what life changing context looks like in a small discipleship group and how Jesus created it.

3- How did Jesus bring about transformation in the men he discipled?

4- How important is leadership development to the movement of Christianity? How did Jesus develop leaders?

5- Explain "heart" and how important it is in leadership development.

6- Read Jeremiah 3:15. How could this verse be a prophecy that was fulfilled in Jesus?

7- How well is your church raising up new leaders that are disciple making leaders?

DAY TWENTY-TWO

"Language Shapes Culture"

Maybe you have heard the phrase, "language shapes culture". Nothing could be truer for an organization. The language that you use affects what any organization will become, so choose your language carefully.

If the mission of the church is to "make disciples of all nations", then I would argue that the church needs disciple making language. I can honestly say that the church where I have been pastoring for the past thirty years is saturated with the language of disciple making. Our mission statement is "to be and build disciples", our lobby is filled with images of a "fully trained disciple", and every message usually has a reference that connects to disciple making. If people do what people hear, then they are going to hear about disciple making at our church.

Even Jesus used language to shape a disciple making culture. The word disciple is used 269 times in the Gospels and Acts and Jesus clearly called his disciples to be disciples and make disciples. The early church was not debating what the mission was or what it looked like when they accomplished it. They had very clear marching orders to make disciples that looked and acted like Jesus.

I find it interesting how many times I speak on disciple making and people, even pastors, confide in me that they have never heard this disciple making stuff before. Can you imagine a restaurant that never talks about the menu? Would an athletic team never discuss the playbook or game plan? Do you think a school system would never have planning sessions to discuss curriculum? You get the point. Organizations talk about the things that relate to the mission if they plan on fulfilling it. Only in the church do you find people never or rarely talking about the very thing Jesus did and how he did it.

In the last week of this Thirty-Day booklet I am going to share with you the language we use in the church that I lead. It is not the only language or even the best language, but it is language that drives the mission. I encourage you to come up with your own language or use ours. If it helps you drive the mission of Jesus, have at it. You don't even have to give us credit as long as it is used for making disciples of Jesus!

DIG DEEPER

Read **Psalm 78:1-8** and write any observations that you discover.

_____
_____
_____

DAY TWENTY-THREE

"Mission Language"

No one would be surprised to hear Super Bowl talk in an NFL locker room. No one would be shocked to hear World Series talk in an MLB clubhouse. You would certainly expect discussions on National Championships in a college football field house. A political convention would be filled with discussions about their candidate's run for office. I could go on and on. The point is the church should be filled with the language of making disciples.

In one of the last statements Jesus made, Matthew 28:19 and 20, he made the mission of "making disciples of all nations" incredibly clear. Jesus was not stuttering when he told the original disciples, to be about the business of making disciples until he returned. Give that, we should never get tired of talking about what it means to be a disciple and make more disciples. That mission language should permeate everything we do.

Jesus did not only tell us to make disciples, he also defined what a disciple is supposed to look like. In Luke 6:40 Jesus said, *"A disciple is not above his teacher, but everyone when he is fully trained will be like his teacher."* Jesus clearly instructed us to make disciples that look like him. We don't make disciples that look like Peter, James, or John. We make fully trained disciples that have the character and conduct of Christ.

In the church where I pastor you will constantly hear two phrases. We constantly talk bout the mission of "being and building" disciples and we constantly talk about leading untrained seekers to become "fully trained" disciples. The goal is for everyone that regularly attends or belongs to our church to have laser like focus when it comes to knowing what our mission is.

If the mission is ambiguous you are not very likely to hit it. If the mission is confusing, don't expect to fulfill it. If the mission is never talked about, you won't accomplish it. Make the language of the mission clear, consistent, and compelling.

<u>Clear</u>: Jesus told his disciples exactly what to do till he came back. he also did it with them so they would have no question about his instructions.

<u>Consistent</u>: The mission of Jesus has not changed in over two thousand years. It remains the same!

<u>Compelling</u>: The mission of Jesus is worth giving up your life for. There is no higher calling than to make disciples of Jesus.

DIG DEEPER

Read **Habakkuk 2:2-3** and write down an insight or two about what you read.

_____
_____
_____

DAY TWENTY-FOUR

"Target Language"

When you take a newborn baby to the doctor they will always weigh and measure that baby. They will actually continue to do this even with adults. For a child, however, they use those measurements to compare a baby to a percentile of how other children have developed over hundreds of years. The doctor will compare your child's growth to other children by using a chart on the wall. That chart becomes a consistent target for objectively evaluating a child's growth and development. You do not want a doctor that simply guesses at your child's growth.

Making disciples and spiritual growth and development is in many ways like measuring babies. We can actually compare the character and conduct of a disciple with every "fully trained" disciple since the time of Christ. The Bible becomes the chart on the wall if you will. The Bible gives clear and objective qualities of Christ's character and conduct. Those objective qualities need to be the language in your church.

In the church where I am pastor we refer to a "fully trained" disciple as an M-7 Disciple. That means we are seeking to develop disciples that have seven marks of a disciple that are all seen in Christ and every one of his disciples. Our goal is to develop disciples that are members, magnifiers, maturing, ministers, managers, messengers, and multipliers. We also seek to develop disciples that demonstrate love, joy, peace, patience, kindness, goodness, gentleness, faithfulness, and self control. Regardless of what you call it, be sure the product you are working to develop is a fully trained disciple that looks and acts like Jesus.

I am sure you can identify many more marks of s disciple than we use but the key is to know what it looks like when you have actually filled the mission. if you don't know what your target is you will never know if you hit it. If you do not have target language you will never know if you hit or even know that you have one.

When you read the first description of the church given in Acts 2:42-47 you are also reading the description of the disciples and Jesus. Their conduct was reproducible and it became the chart on the wall for making disciples. The church in Acts did not describe a disciple with "M" words but they were a community of people becoming like Jesus. Even Paul was talking about being like Christ in 1 Corinthians 11:1. No doubt Paul was a fully trained disciple.

DIG DEEPER

Read **1 Thessalonians 1:8,9** and write a thought or two.

_____
_____
_____

Multiplier · Member · Magnifier · Minister · Maturing · Manager · Messenger

- Love
- Joy
- Peace
- Patience
- Kindness
- Goodness
- Faithfulness
- Gentleness
- Self-Control

DAY TWENTY-FIVE

"Strategy Language"

Have you ever realized that a blueprint is "how to" language. A set of blueprints actually tells you how to build a house, a building or any object. Blueprints for making something serve as a strategy for construction. A good set of prints gives you a design or a pattern to follow in building whatever you are attempting to build. Blueprints are a good thing to have. They help a builder build the right thing and build it in the right way!

Jesus gave his disciples a blueprint for making disciples. The way Jesus lived and the way he made the original disciples has become the pattern for all other disciples. We don't need a new blueprint; Jesus' blueprint still works. Jesus is the model disciple and disciple maker. His strategy is the only strategy we will ever need to make disciples of all nations that are fully trained.

In the church where I serve, we call the strategy of Jesus the "funnel". On the following page is a graphic illustrating what it looks like. The funnel is our blueprint for how we help lead untrained seekers to become fully trained disciples. We do it today the exact same way Jesus did it two thousand years ago. We don't need the latest and greatest methods of making disciples; we need what has been tried, tested, and true for over two thousand years.

We have updated and summarized some words to help communicate the strategy Jesus used. For "come and see" we use the words *reach-out*. For "come and behold" we use the words *lift-up*. For "come and follow" we use the words *plug-in*. To describe "come and remain" we use the words *build-up*. To explain "come and go" we use the phrase *send-out*. The words have been updated and modernized. They are even easy to say and remember, but the meaning is the same as they were two thousand years ago. The funnel is the language we use to communicate the strategy of Jesus.

Every church needs to have a strategy. That strategy needs to be the same one Jesus used. You don't need a new strategy, you simply need to figure out how you are going to say it.

Once you figure out the language you will use for Christ's strategy you need to get everyone speaking the same language. Remember the Tower of Babel couldn't be completed because God confused their language. When it comes to the Great Commission God wants the opposite. He wants everyone saying the same thing and doing the same thing. The right language will help make that happen.

DIG DEEPER

Read **2 Timothy 2:2** and write down any observations you might have.

_____
_____
_____

DAY TWENTY-SIX

"Environment Language"

Hang out in a gym or fitness center and you will hear some things you don't hear anywhere else. You will hear talk of reps, sets, and workout routines. There is a unique language used in fitness centers. If you hang out in an automotive garage you will hear a different type of language. You will hear words like gears, gauges, and gaskets. Mechanics have their own language. Spend some time in a school classroom and you'll discover teachers and students use a common language. Words like tests, homework, and grades are words they all understand.

In the local church we should also have a common language for disciple making environments. Words like information, application, accountability, relationships, and fellowship should be words we use to describe the environments used for making disciples. There should be words that describe life in a large group, life in a small group, and life doing ministry with each other. The New Testament is filled with the words used for environments.

At the church where I serve as pastor we use some very specific words to help describe the environments we use for making disciples. When we encourage people to attend a worship service we are inviting them into a large group which is somewhat similar to when Jesus taught on a mountainside. When we ask people to join a "Community Group" we are encouraging them to join a small group similar to what we believe was described as a home group in the Jerusalem church. When we challenge people to join an "Impact group" this is language we use to call people into a small discipleship group where they learn the character and conduct of

Christ. When we speak about joining a "Ministry Team" we are asking people to find a place to serve in or through our church. Our language is very specific to our church, and yet it communicates the same environments that Jesus used two thousand years ago.

The goal for "environment language" is to choose whatever language helps you to communicate where people need to be. if people are unclear about the environments they need to be in, you cannot get upset when they are not there!

People in our church regularly hear me say, "you need to participate in corporate worship". They hear me say, "everyone needs to be in a Community group". They hear me encourage people to "join an Impact group". I often talk about "becoming part of a Ministry team". I try to use consistent language to help point people in the right direction. Choose the language that will help you lead people to become fully trained disciples.

DIG DEEPER

Read **Genesis 11:1-9**. Write any insights you have.

_____
_____
_____

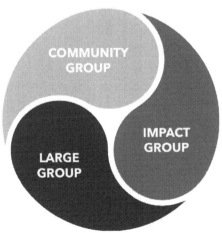

DAY TWENTY-SEVEN

"Leadership Language"

A while back I read a bumper sticker on the back of a car that said, "Lead, follow, or get the heck out of the way". To be truthful, heck was not the word it used.

That bumper sticker started me thinking about the importance of being sure leaders are leading in the right direction. I wasn't truly following that driver, but if I had been, the question was- did he know where he was going? It is important to have leaders, but even more important to have leaders that are leading in the right direction.

The church needs to have disciple making leaders. If all we talk about is having leaders, we are speaking the wrong language. We need disciple making leaders because disciple making is the mission of the church. If you are in a church with leadership development that is not developing disciple making leaders you have the wrong process! I am amazed at how many churches are using the secular world as the basis for leadership development, rather than scripture, and wondering why we don't have disciple making leaders in place.

I like the leadership language of the Bible more than the business model. This brings me back to Jeremiah 3:15, *"I will give you shepherds after my own heart, that will lead you with knowledge and understanding."* (NIV) The biblical model of leadership is to have leaders that have a heart after God and that know and understand how to lead like Jesus did. We use this language because Jesus was a leader with a heart after God and had the knowledge and understanding for how to make disciples.

Jesus was the perfect disciple making leader and he was focused on leading toward the mission of making disciples of all nations. Perhaps one of the greatest problems in the church these days is that we have leaders that are not being developed out of discipleship and for the right mission?

In the church where I serve we use the language of a 315 Leader continually. We use that language because it defines what we believe a disciple making leader is made of. The right heart, right knowledge, and right understanding. We also use a curriculum we developed to help equip a fully trained disciple to serve as a disciple making leader. We use 315 to help us with leader development rather than leadership development. The 315 curriculum helps a person become the right person more than developing the skills and abilities of leading. Leader development focuses on the person. Leadership development focuses on the task. Make sure you have the right language for your leaders.

DIG DEEPER

Read **Titus 1:5-9** and write any insights you have.

_____
_____
_____

DAY TWENTY-EIGHT

"The Curriculum of Disciple Making"

Let's be clear, if language shapes culture you need to have a discipleship curriculum that speaks the right language. That curriculum is the Word of God!

The only disciple making curriculum that will change and transform a person's life is the Bible. The Bible is the inspired and inerrant Word of God, and it has the power to change a person's life. It can take a person from an untrained seeker and make that person into a world changing disciple. Only the bible can have that kind of impact.

I do believe, however, that it helps to have some discipleship resource that helps to get us into the bible. Especially when it comes to learning what the bible says about the character and conduct of Christ. Every word in the scriptures is inspired and important but it helps to have a tool that helps us understand certain parts of the bible better.

As a pastor who has been unapologetically committed to leading the church to make disciples, I decided to develop a curriculum to help make that process easier. I have written a disciple making curriculum called the *Impact Series*. It is a curriculum designed to help get people into God's Word so they can see what it means to be and build disciples. It does not teach you everything you can know, but it teaches you what you need to know in order to be a disciple and build more disciples of Christ.

It is my conviction after thirty years of pastoring that a church needs to settle on discipleship curriculum that is both biblical and reproducible. A biblical curriculum helps you consolidate the key ingredients of disciple making out of the life of Christ. A reproducible curriculum provides a tool that can be consistently used from one generation of disciples to the next. If you keep changing curriculum it will be hard to reproduce disciples.

The curriculum we use at the discipleship level of our church is designed to give people a foundation of discipleship essentials. Teach people the character of Christ, the conduct of Christ, and what it means to be a 315 leader like Christ. Our curriculum uses the language we see in the scriptures when it comes to making disciples the way Jesus made disciples.

I encourage you to check out the Impact Series and some of our other resources on our website, impactdisciples.com, and find a curriculum to use in your church that is both biblical and reproducible.

DIG DEEPER

Read **Acts 17:5-8** and make an observation or two about the passage.

_____
_____
_____

The Impact Series
impactdisciples.com

DAY TWENTY-NINE

"The Making of a Disciple Making Pastor"

Maybe you've heard the phrase, "The speed of the leader equals the speed of the team"? There is so much truth in that well-worn phrase and especially when it comes to the role of the pastor within the local church. The speed of the pastor will affect the speed of the church in accomplishing the mission of Christ.

If the speed of the pastor is critical to mission success, then every church needs to have a disciple making pastor. Having a disciple making pastor is not a guarantee. A disciple making pastor is not a given. It is not automatic. Disciple making pastors are made, not born.

One of the problems in the church today is that pastors are not typically trained to be disciple makers. Often times the models most pastors learn under are not disciple makers and most seminaries do not teach disciple making. Most pastors become what they hear and see and more often than not they don't see or hear much about disciple making. I know that was true for me and I believe it is true for the vast majority of other pastors.

I am so thankful that shortly after graduating from seminary and planting a church the Lord exposed me to the principles of disciple making and the priorities of a disciple making pastor. Decades later I feel a burden to share those principles and priorities with other pastors and church planters.

A few years ago I started an online equipping group called *The Making of a Disciple Making Pastor* in hopes of helping as many pastors as possible learn the priorities we see in Jesus for leading a movement of multiplying disciples. We now have an entire team of people leading these groups and we hope to put a dent in the need for pastors that know how to lead disciple making churches.

The *Making of a Disciple Making Pastor* includes the following six priorities of Jesus.

Leading toward mission
Leading self first
Leading the church or organization
Leading leaders
Leading with a plan
Leading well

Learning those six priorities combined with relationships and accountability will help any pastor grow and begin to discover what it means to be a disciple making pastor.

DIG DEEPER

Read **John 17:4** and make an observation about that verse.

_____
_____
_____

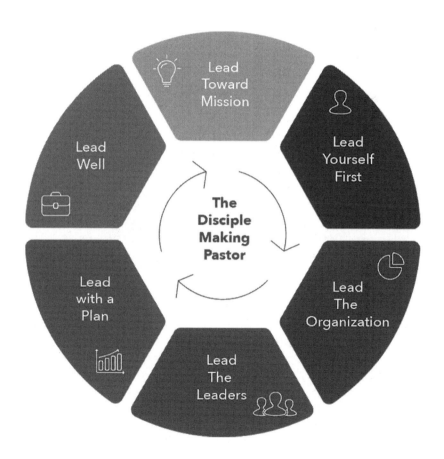

DAY TWENTY-THIRTY

"The Making of a Disciple Making Church"

I have often told people that the book I need to write someday is, *"How not to build a disciple making church"*. After thirty years of trial and error, I can honestly say I know a lot more of what "not to do" to build a disciple making church than what "to do".

I am so grateful that God allowed me to plant a church with leadership that was willing to let me try lots of things when it comes to disciple making. The church where I pastor has actually become a laboratory for disciple making. We have had the freedom to try many different approaches to the concept of making disciples. It has been a great journey, and I believe we are closer to figuring it out today than we ever have been.

Our church still has a long way to go in learning what it means to be a disciple making church, but we are making progress and we do have more clarity in that process than ever. Having said that, we are also at a point where we are trying to help other churches figure it out as well. We have learned enough that we are now able to help others get started in that same process. Much of what you have read in this booklet are the principles we have discovered over the past thirty years. Hopefully it will jump start you on a journey of disciple making as well.

Now that you have read *The First Thirty Days to Becoming a Disciple Making Church* I hope you are more committed than ever to that pursuit. If you are, Impact Ministries would love the chance to come alongside you and help you learn more about the elements of a disciple making church. We actually lead a seminar called the Disciple Making Church Seminar that teaches the four key ingredients that Jesus used to build a disciple making movement.

A clear target
A consistent strategy
A life -changing environment
A called leadership

Impact Ministries has a team of trainers that are able to come and conduct a *Disciple Making Church Seminar* in your local church or with other churches in your area. We also provide consultation and coaching when it comes to becoming a church committed to disciple making. Check out ***impactdisciples.com*** for all the information you need about the seminar and all the other resources we offer to help churches be and build disciples.

DIG DEEPER

Read **Acts 1:8** and record any insights have you on this verse.

_____
_____
_____

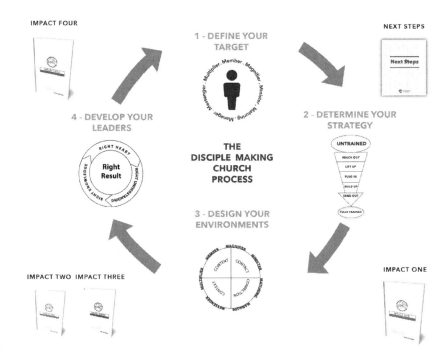

QUESTIONS FOR REFLECTION OR DISCUSSION

The past nine days has hopefully helped you understand more of what it means to have a Disciple Making Church. Take a few minutes to reflect on the following questions or discuss them with others.

1- Take a minute and discuss the language of your church and the type of culture you currently have. How does your language need to change?

2- How well do the people in your church know the mission of the church and the target of the church?

3- How would you evaluate the way your church is executing the strategy Jesus used to make disciples? What can you do differently?

4- Describe any discipleship environments you've been in and how they are similar or different from what Jesus created.

5- How would you evaluate the leadership development priority and process in your church? What, if anything, needs to change?

6- How important is the Pastor's role in helping the church make disciples?

7- What are the next steps you see your church taking to become a disciple making church? How could Impact Ministries help you?

Made in the USA
Columbia, SC
10 November 2021